POETRY SAFARI

The South East

Edited By Sarah Washer

First published in Great Britain in 2017 by:

YoungWriters Est. 1991

Coltsfoot Drive
Peterborough
PE2 9BF
Telephone: 01733 890066
Website: www.youngwriters.co.uk

Book Design by Spencer Hart

SB ISBN 978-1-78624-736-0
Printed and bound in the UK by BookPrintingUK
Website: www.bookprintinguk.com
YB0298H

Foreword

Welcome, Reader, to 'Poetry Safari – The South East'.

For Young Writers' latest poetry competition, we asked our writers to go wild and write a poem about their favourite animal, whether it's hidden in the depths of the ocean, swinging through the jungle, or curled up next to them on the sofa.

The result is this collection of fantastic poetic verse that covers a whole host of different topics. Get your explorer gear ready as you discover friendly fish and deep sea creatures, whacky zoo wildlife from mischievous monkeys to funny flamingos, and even cuddly cats and other domestic pets. You may even spot a unicorn or other mythical beast! This collection has a poem to suit everyone.

Whereas the majority of our writers chose to stick to a free verse style, others gave themselves the added challenge of writing in acrostic form.

There was a great response to this competition which is always nice to see, and the standard of entries was excellent, therefore I'd like to thank everyone who entered in their poems and showed us their wild side!

I hope you enjoy reading these poems as much as I did.

Keep writing,
Sarah Washer

Contents

The Poems

What Am I?

I have big ears.
I am white.
I am fluffy.
I nibble carrots.
I hop a lot.
What am I?

Emily Drake (6)
Great Gaddesden CE Primary School, Hemel Hempstead

What Am I?

I look like a yummy sausage.
I am as long as a sausage.
I have long floppy ears.
What am I?

Fallon Makepeace (6)
Great Gaddesden CE Primary School, Hemel Hempstead

What Am I?

I have a spotty tail.
I have spots on my body.
I am tall.
What am I?

Sebastian Blomley (6)
Great Gaddesden CE Primary School, Hemel Hempstead

The Snake

The snake is very long.
The snake is very colourful but when I am next to him he wriggles about.
The snake is very dangerous and when he is eating food he is as cold as the freezer.
The snake is very terrifying when he is in the spooky garden.
The snake is very green.

Diana Cristina Marin (6)
Larchfield Primary School, Maidenhead

My Ferocious Doggy

My ferocious dog likes to catch thieves.
When we go for a walk, if anyone runs in front of him,
He gets as angry as a porcupine.
When he see a police car he says, 'Woof, woof, woof'
Which means, 'Can I have a ride in your car?'

Sakshi Suji (6)
Larchfield Primary School, Maidenhead

My Cat

I have a cat,
My cat is powerful, silly and little.
My cat looks like lavender and yellow sunflowers.
My cat likes to eat mice, meat and milk.
My cat likes to think of an enormous mouse and amazing milk.

Oliwia Przybylo (6)
Larchfield Primary School, Maidenhead

If I Had A Cat

If I had a cat I could dance all day.
If I had a cat I could play all day.
If I had a cat I could eat all day.
If I had a cat I could walk all day.
If I had a cat I could jump all day.

Myra Khan Raza (6)
Larchfield Primary School, Maidenhead

The Talented Horse

My horse is very talented,
He can juggle.
My horse is talented,
He can canter very fast.
My horse is talented,
He can jump the highest jump without any poles off.

Amy Lillywhite (6)
Larchfield Primary School, Maidenhead

My Snake

My snake plays on the bed.
My snake eats meat.
My snake rattles every day.
My snake lives in my house.
My snake loves me.
My snake helps me.
My snake is good.

Benjamin Honig (6)
Larchfield Primary School, Maidenhead

The Talented Monkey

Talented monkey climbed.
Talented monkey found a banana.
Talented monkey gave me a huggle.
Talented monkey is as soft as an owl.
Talented monkey smells like flowers.

Morgan Steadman White (6)
Larchfield Primary School, Maidenhead

Frog

The frog stinks, he smells like rotten fish.
The frog looks green and sticky.
The frog croaks loudly.
The frog jumps under water.
The frog is slimy and crinkly.

Lourena Dala (7)
Larchfield Primary School, Maidenhead

If I Had Claws Like A Crab

If I had claws I could pinch people.
If I had claws I could pinch other fish.
If I had claws I could grab seaweed.
If I had claws I could grab hold of something.

Rupert Mattia-Ruggiero (7)
Larchfield Primary School, Maidenhead

My Magic Snake

My snake has magic powers.
My snake is golden, shiny and sparkling.
My snake is a he.
My snake can climb high buildings.
I have my snake in the house.

Leonardo Patrinos (6)

Larchfield Primary School, Maidenhead

My Owl

My owl flies in the wind with a tin of yummy
worms.
My owl makes its babies cosy.
My owl is white and brown.
He likes to play peek-a-boo with his babies.

Leighton Porter (7)
Larchfield Primary School, Maidenhead

Rattlesnake

My rattle snake is noisy.
My rattle snake is enormous.
I see my dangerous, enormous rattle snake
every day.
It is a colourful rattle snake.

Leandro Tobli (6)
Larchfield Primary School, Maidenhead

My Lizard

My lizard can eat.
He can run really fast.
He loves lots of meat,
And can count to ten.
He is beautiful with his pattern.

Milana Kotlyarova (6)
Larchfield Primary School, Maidenhead

The Rabbit Is Greedy

The rabbit is greedy.
At night he hops through the window.
He opens the fridge, there is a sparkly, shiny carrot,
He eats it!

Tia louise Wetherall (7)
Larchfield Primary School, Maidenhead

The Snake

My snake is stripy.
My snake is dangerous.
My snake is stinky.
My snake is funny.
My snake lives in the cave.

Jack Goddard (6)
Larchfield Primary School, Maidenhead

Golden Door

The sky was blue, it was a beautiful day.
The sun was out and Ella the unicorn had
just had her delicious dinner,
It was macaroni and cheese, so yummy.
Now she was eating a lovely desert, it was
candyfloss and jelly, it was very yummy for
Ella the unicorn.
Then she went to play hopscotch with her
friends Piskey, Tegen and Connor.
They were very good friends to Ella the
unicorn.
She always plays with her best friend too,
Renee.

Renee Ava Nichols (6)
Newlands Primary School, Ramsgate

Glitzy Squirrel

Olivia is a silly squirrel.
Olivia is little bit bossy with small eyebrows.
Olivia is clever and has spots.
Olivia has got good eyes because she can see in the darkness.
Olivia is brown and pink in the ears.
She is the prettiest squirrel ever.
Olivia is never in shows.
Olivia is so, so, so kind and nice.
Her favourite foods are nuts and candyfloss.
Olivia is a little bit bad, she is told off for fighting.

Ella Louise Lawrence (6)
Newlands Primary School, Ramsgate

The Sad Squirrel

One day there was a squirrel, his name was Huburt.
He didn't have any friends or family.
He was bored so he came to a person with a lovely voice and said,
'A man with no hair has a life of despair.'
'Thank you for telling me that.'
But another person came up and said,
'Try this, singing.'

Leila-Rose Kelly (6)
Newlands Primary School, Ramsgate

Happy Cat

One day there was a cat
The cat was walking in the forest
She was far from home and she found a gingerbread house
The cat knocked on the door but no one answered
The cat decided that she would go inside the gingerbread house
Suddenly a witch came back to her home
It was the gingerbread house
The cat hid...

Ryder Walker (6)
Newlands Primary School, Ramsgate

The Cat That Sits

A cat tastes a lot of biscuits
Stripy and brown, its name is Catrific
It drinks out of a bowl
It walks around
It bounces a lot
It scratches, it bites
It sits on the windowsill
It looks out the window
It sits a lot and in a lot of places.

Connor Stephen John Warren (6)
Newlands Primary School, Ramsgate

The Dream Of Magic

Once upon a time there was a lovely unicorn
Who loved to share with friends.
One day she went up to bed and fell asleep
And had a dream.
She had a dream about a magic land,
It was beautiful.
Sadly she woke up in shock.

Madalyn Louise Cogger (8)
Newlands Primary School, Ramsgate

Pink Fluffy Unicorn

It flies and it is pink.
It has got golden wings, a rainbow horn
And it likes to eat rainbow grass.
It lives in a castle and it likes to go to the wood
And play with its friends.

Tyler Bellenie (6)
Newlands Primary School, Ramsgate

The Silly Elephant

My elephant is silly and grey.
She lives in a shelter.
My elephant eats bananas and apples.
She plays with water and squirts it!
She runs around squirting at people.

Lily Mar Noble (6)
Newlands Primary School, Ramsgate

Untitled

The little bunny is a big mess
And he is messy.
He is a very soft bunny
And he is a really nice bunny.
He is really soft when I hug him.
Bunnies are cuddly.

Olivia Serafin (7)
Newlands Primary School, Ramsgate

Butterfly Senses

It smells beautiful.
It looks pretty.
Butterflies sound like ballerinas dancing through the air.
Butterflies feel like silk.
Butterflies taste like fresh mints.

Daisy Ball (6)
Newlands Primary School, Ramsgate

Dog Show Is Open Every Day

Snake and dog, you are going to be in a circus!
The dog eats lots of food.
My dog eats pasta.
My dog lives on a rainbow.
The snake eats crocs.

Tommy Rayner
Newlands Primary School, Ramsgate

Penguin

The penguin is smelly like rotten eggs
And he eats fish because they are good.
He tastes like smelly socks.
He feels happy and soft.

Lilly Clark (6)
Newlands Primary School, Ramsgate

The Penguin In Space

The penguin bounces a lot.
The penguin lives on ice.
The penguin is shiny.
The penguin went to another planet!

Brandon Fisher
Newlands Primary School, Ramsgate

The Super Dog

My super dog can do anything in the whole world.
My dog likes to go to the plane for rides.
He likes paper.

Zak Read (7)
Newlands Primary School, Ramsgate

Rhino

He eats lots of food.
He eats apples that disappear.
My animal is grey.
My rhino likes to charge!

Jake Wharton (7)
Newlands Primary School, Ramsgate

Crazy Creature

My crazy creature smells like body wash
Sounds like thunder
Feels like a big fluffy teddy.

William M Cody (6)
Newlands Primary School, Ramsgate

Fluffy Puffy

My polar bear loves playing with her friends.
She loves eating.
I love my polar bear.

Mia Harris (6)
Newlands Primary School, Ramsgate

Untitled

He lives in a tree.
He eats meat.
He is yellow.
What animal is he?

Charlie John Robert Hendry (6)
Newlands Primary School, Ramsgate

Tiger

It is as stripy as a zebra,
Its teeth are as sharp as a shark's teeth,
It is as fluffy as a cat,
It is yellow like gold.
It's black like the night,
It's as white as snow,
It runs like a cheetah,
It's amazing.
It's beautiful,
It's scary,
It tastes like chocolate cake,
It's as ferocious as a rhino.

Beth Cox (6)
Oakley CE Combined School, Aylesbury

Tiger

With killer speed,
Stamping on every weed,
It kills what it needs,
Breaks down the trees.
Spying on what it needs,
Pouncing on what it sees,
Darting through the leaves.
Leaves go up,
Leaves go down,
Killing nature all around.

Nathaniel Hemmings (7)
Oakley CE Combined School, Aylesbury

Tiger

A tiger is as stripy as a zebra in the shadows creeping
Slowly in the dark it leaves quickly for the park.
A tiger is as fast as a cheetah running like the wind
Prowling around its prey as quickly as it can.

Ophelia May Cayzer (6)
Oakley CE Combined School, Aylesbury

Tigers

Tiger's bodies are orange like a rainbow.
Tiger's stripes are as black as the night.
Tiger's teeth are as sharp as a knife.
Their claws are as sharp as a shark's teeth.

Beatrix Gurney (5)
Oakley CE Combined School, Aylesbury

Cat

A cat is as soft as a marshmallow.
A cat's teeth are as sharp as a saw.
It's as fast as a fox.
It's claws are as sharp as a shark's tooth.

Megan Dollah (6)
Oakley CE Combined School, Aylesbury

Elephant

An elephant is grey like a rain cloud.
Its trunk is as long as a snake.
An elephant is big.
An elephant has a long trunk.
It squirts water out.

Ophelia Beaumont-Hill (5)
Oakley CE Combined School, Aylesbury

Tiger

The tiger has teeth as sharp as nails,
And the tiger lives in the woods when it's
dark.
A tiger roars when he wakes up.
The tiger scratches its head.

Frederick Pratt (6)

Oakley CE Combined School, Aylesbury

Snake

Blood suckers like vampires,
Slippery as a fish,
As scary as a shark,
With dangerous fangs,
Scaly like lizards.
Hissing through the grass.

Billy George Smith (7)
Oakley CE Combined School, Aylesbury

Tiger

A tiger is as vicious as a bear.
A tiger is as black as a cat.
A tiger is quiet like a mouse.
It sits quietly and sleeps.

Tiffany Olalekan (6)
Oakley CE Combined School, Aylesbury

Tiger

A tiger's teeth are as sharp as a knife.
It's as furry as a dog.
As furry as a leopard.
A tiger is scary.

Harriet Gallagher (5)
Oakley CE Combined School, Aylesbury

Tiger

A tiger is as sharp as a knife
A tiger is as hairy as a dog.
A tiger is as fast as a leopard.
As soft as a cat.

Stephanie Olalekan (6)
Oakley CE Combined School, Aylesbury

Tiger

A tiger has teeth,
It is as furry as a cat,
The tiger's teeth are sharper than a needle,
The tiger is scary.

Eva Roberts (5)
Oakley CE Combined School, Aylesbury

Tiger

A tiger is a scary creature.
It is orange with black stripes.

Daisy Veness (5)
Oakley CE Combined School, Aylesbury

Tigger The Tiger

Tigger the tiger trapped a toenail under the bathroom door
He tripped and he slipped,
He skidded and flipped,
Ending up in a pile on the floor!
Then out came a mouse from his hiding place,
Tigger the tiger saw his cheeky rodent face,
'Get up!' squeaked the mouse,
'This isn't cool. If you don't go now you'll be late for school!'

Isabella Calnilia May Ashead-Jones (7)
Portway Primary School, London

Cheetah

Spotty like my scarf,
As soft as a cloud,
Dangerous like a lion,
As fast as lightning,
In the morning it sneaks out,
And catches all the animals lurking about.
Whiskers long and thin,
Teeth sharp like shards,
As scary as a shark,
As silly as a monkey,
And as lazy as a lion.
Runs miles all over the place.

Sonali Arora Pasco (7)
Portway Primary School, London

Leopard

Faster than a racing car,
Slower than a cheetah.
It hunts at night,
We need to look out,
Before they come near!
They only eat meat.
Be careful!
Oh dear!
It runs as fast as lightning,
Fifty-eight miles per hour!

Oscar Andersson Allen (7)
Portway Primary School, London

The Kitten

I scratch, I claw
With my miniature paws.
I have eyes like two tiny tropical pools.
When I'm older I'll go out in the garden.
I sleep a lot but that's what kittens do.
I am a mammal just like you.

Amelia Kubas (6)
Portway Primary School, London

The Tiger

T akes on all and always wins
I nstinctive and highly intelligent
G oes across the Savannah like a lightning bolt
E ats only meat for he's a carnivore
R oars as loud as thunder

Olivia Alla Hernandez (6)
Portway Primary School, London

Cat

Laying on the sofa,
Making a miaow noise.
She is black and scary.
Her laser eyes are looking,
Whiskers white and sharp.
She walks around my room
And scares a little mouse.

Stefan Bobeanu (6)
Portway Primary School, London

If I Were

If I were a cat
I would eat little, grey mice.
I would play with a crunchy brown leaf.
I would do nothing at all, all day long.
I would climb knobbly trees.
I would catch little, brown birds.
And bring them home with me.
I would love to have cuddles and hugs.

Florence Stott (6)
St Andrew's School, Bedford

My Bunny

My bunny's name is Lily
She is very funny
My bunny's eyes are brown
My bunny runs to me
Whenever she sees me
My bunny climbs on new people
But when I leave the house
She scratches my wall
So I tell her to go back in her cage

Cozette Liljenquist (6)
St Andrew's School, Bedford

If I Were A Spider

If I were a spider
I would get stepped on.
If I were a spider
I would run away.
If I were a spider
I would eat flies.
If I were a spider
I would get washed down the sink.
If I were a spider
I would be scared of people.

Scarlett McCormack (6)
St Andrew's School, Bedford

Snakes

A snake smells like dead mice.
A snake looks green and yellow.
A snake tastes like jelly.
A snake feels scaly like a fish.
A snake sounds like a hissing kettle.

Freda Brown (6)
St Andrew's School, Bedford

My Pet Monkey

My pet monkey likes to swing on trees
My pet monkey is brown
He likes to eat ripe bananas
My pet monkey has long hands
My pet monkey smells like leaves

Deborah Nyantowo (6)
St Andrew's School, Bedford

If I Were...

If I were a bee
I would collect nectar
From a flower
And bring it to the hive
To make honey
I would sting people
If I was scared

Rosalia Hendry (6)
St Andrew's School, Bedford

About Lions And Foxes

Lions are strong, they like to eat meat and it is yummy.
It's good for them, it's very sweet.
I love lions, I wish I had a lion that doesn't bite me.
I want a happy lion, not an angry lion.
It could bite me but I'm not afraid of lions.
A fox is strong too.
I'm very brave, be brave too.
Don't be scared for foxes won't bite.

Daniel Kufre-Obot (6)
St Cyprian's Greek Orthodox Primary Academy, Thornton Heath

The Cat And Tiger

C at is very soft
A t home it likes to purr
T he tail of the cat is very soft and pretty

T he tiger is very stripy
I like tigers
G rowling tigers are very cross
E ating meat and other animals
R ainy days are when they don't go out

Molly
St Cyprian's Greek Orthodox Primary Academy, Thornton Heath

The Princess And The Owl

The princess was walking and found an owl,
It was sparkly, they became friends.
One day something was rustling in the bushes,
It was a monster, the princess was frightened.
The owl ran and got help,
They went home together.

Tiarna Clarke (6)
St Cyprian's Greek Orthodox Primary Academy, Thornton Heath

Cat Poem

C uddly and curious
A happy girl
T he cat likes meat

P erfect company
O utdoors playing hide-and-seek
E yes are big and beautiful
M y best friend

Miranda Sophia Tsoukkas (6)
St Cyprian's Greek Orthodox Primary Academy, Thornton Heath

The Princess Cat

The prince's cat had a shining tail, it was so majestic.
She was very adventurous.
One day she saw a hat and it was like her hat.
She ran as fast as she could and cats came to to help her.

Rahzia Boreland (7)
St Cyprian's Greek Orthodox Primary Academy, Thornton Heath

Catfish

My fish can slip and whip and flap on the ground.
Sometimes in the morning he leaves the house and plays with his friends.
When I go to the sea he squirts at me and I squirt back at him!

Jamaine Gonzales (6)
St Cyprian's Greek Orthodox Primary Academy, Thornton Heath

Lion Time

L ion run, lion run before you get hit by
lightning
I t roars, it won't fish
O h, rooooar! It got hit by lightning!
N ow it roars for nice fish!

Alexei Midnight Grunhard (6)
St Cyprian's Greek Orthodox Primary Academy, Thornton Heath

Lion

L is for lion, it eats meat
I is for insects, that's what it thinks it likes
O is for obedient, it obeys someone
N is for needle-like claws

Irina Gusarova (6)
St Cyprian's Greek Orthodox Primary Academy, Thornton Heath

Dolphin Sophia

Dolphins like to splash.
Dolphins like swimming.
Dophins like to eat fish.
Dolphins like to squirt.
Dolphins like the little fishes.

Melissa Coulloupas (6)
St Cyprian's Greek Orthodox Primary Academy, Thornton Heath

Bird Flying In The Sky

One day a bird flew to the sky
And then landed on the green
He saw a huge cat that nearly ate the bird
But he flew away, off the ground

Georgios Gkorogias (6)
St Cyprian's Greek Orthodox Primary Academy, Thornton Heath

Fish Poem

F ood is its favourite thing
I nteresting and swimming
S parkly and pretty
H appy because it gets fed

Ksenia Tsambika Nestoros (5)
St Cyprian's Greek Orthodox Primary Academy, Thornton Heath

A Poem About Leopards

I like leopards because they are sweet and very cuddly to me.
I like leopards because they are very clean, nice and very good.

Feno Omoma (6)

St Cyprian's Greek Orthodox Primary Academy, Thornton Heath

Fish

F riendly and cuddly
I t is always hungry
S wims and swims it does
H ome is where it lives

Ayomide Jemimah Oladimeji (5)
St Cyprian's Greek Orthodox Primary Academy, Thornton Heath

The Bird

My bird is flying and he is laughing.
He sleeps when he is tired.
Then plays again.
He is hidden when he sleeps.

Alonso Rodrigues Ibrahim (6)
St Cyprian's Greek Orthodox Primary Academy, Thornton Heath

Lion

L ion runs
I n the morning lion wakes up
O h no, lion is hurt
N ow lion is sleeping

Nia Biddulph-Harris (6)
St Cyprian's Greek Orthodox Primary Academy, Thornton Heath

Lion Time

L ion lying in the rain
I t is wild
O n the hunt himself
N ow he is asleep

Theo Pavlou (6)
St Cyprian's Greek Orthodox Primary Academy, Thornton Heath

Dog

D ogs can eat really slow
O h no, my dog got hurt
G etting some food, he was hungry

Kaysharna Lee
St Cyprian's Greek Orthodox Primary Academy, Thornton Heath

My Dog

My dog likes to run.
My dog likes to leap.
My dog likes to jump.
My dog likes to eat.

Kaynan Badley (6)
St Cyprian's Greek Orthodox Primary Academy, Thornton Heath

Cat Poem

C ute and little bit friendly
A nd it is nice
T he cat is called Ginger

Eilish Richards (5)
St Cyprian's Greek Orthodox Primary Academy, Thornton Heath

Kitty Poem

C ute and cuddly
A soft and furry cat
T he prettiest and nicest cat

Aaria Sardar (5)
St Cyprian's Greek Orthodox Primary Academy, Thornton Heath

Cat

C ats are clever
A cat is fierce
T hey are cheeky

Ajay Ramdhan
St Cyprian's Greek Orthodox Primary Academy, Thornton Heath

My Dog

A dog smells like mince.
A dog smells tastes like flowers.
A dog looks like a castaway.
My dog feels furry.
A dog sounds like a chatterbox.
A dog is very sleepy.
My dog is very happy.
My dog is a hungry pup.
My dog loves me so much.

Amelia Dawes (5)
Totternhoe Lower School, Dunstable

Dragon

My dragon smells like a fire.
I look and see it has two wings.
It feels like fire.
It sounds like it's breathing fire.
It tastes like beef burgers on the frying pan.

Jack James Norman (5)
Totternhoe Lower School, Dunstable

Shark

My shark has very sharp teeth.
My shark looks like a very big fish.
My shark tastes like a fish.
My shark feels like a soft blanket.
My shark sounds like a chatterbox.

Jake Whitfield (5)
Totternhoe Lower School, Dunstable

Snake

My snake smells rubbery.
My snake looks like a greenfly.
My snake feels soft and slithery.
My snake sounds like 'sssssss'.
My snake tastes like strawberry.

Jamie Ball (5)
Totternhoe Lower School, Dunstable

Dog

My dog smells like mud.
My dog looks round like a fat apple.
My dog tastes like hair.
My dog feels like a feather.
My dog sounds like a chatterbox.

Liam Harvey (5)
Totternhoe Lower School, Dunstable

Lizard

A lizard smells like trainers.
A lizard looks green.
A lizard feels slimy.
A lizard tastes like slime.
A lizard sounds like a snake.

Warami Timeyin-Ayonronmi (5)
Totternhoe Lower School, Dunstable

Dog

A dog smells like smelly socks.
A dog tastes like mud.
A dog feels like furry.
A dog looks like a bear.
A dog sounds like a wail.

Mason McKenzie (5)
Totternhoe Lower School, Dunstable

Cheetah

Smells like stinky trainers.
Looks fast.
Feels soft and fluffy.
Sounds like a fast car.
Tastes like fur.

Isabella Mary Bright (5)
Totternhoe Lower School, Dunstable

Unicorn

Smells like candy and chocolate.
Looks pink and soft.
Feels soft.
Sounds like neighs.
Tastes like candy.

Darcy Dear (5)
Totternhoe Lower School, Dunstable

My Dog

My dog smells like dog food.
Looks fluffy.
Feels like it is soft.
Sounds like barks.
Tastes like fish.

Jessica Hope Allen (5)
Totternhoe Lower School, Dunstable

Cat

Smells like cat food.
Sounds like *miaow*.
Looks like a grey hat.
Feels fluffy.
Tastes yucky.

Fraser Harris (5)
Totternhoe Lower School, Dunstable

Wolf

He smells hairy.
He looks soft.
He feels fluffy.
He sounds loud.
He tastes like a fluffy hamburger.

Scarlett Baulk (5)
Totternhoe Lower School, Dunstable

Mosquito

A mosquito smells like air.
It looks evil.
Sounds like a fly
Tastes like a dead fly.

Joseph Clear (6)
Totternhoe Lower School, Dunstable

Dog

Smells like dirt.
Looks brown.
Feels soft.
Sounds like woof.
Tastes like bones.

Jack Ball (5)
Totternhoe Lower School, Dunstable

Young Writers Information

We hope you have enjoyed reading this book – and that you will continue to in the coming years.

If you're a young writer who enjoys reading and creative writing, or the parent of an enthusiastic poet or story writer, do visit our website www.youngwriters.co.uk. Here you will find free competitions, workshops and games, as well as recommended reads, a poetry glossary and our blog.

If you would like to order further copies of this book, or any of our other titles give us a call or visit **www.youngwriters.co.uk**.

Young Writers, Remus House, Coltsfoot Drive, Peterborough, PER2 9BF
(01733) 890066

info@youngwriters.co.uk